Plant Based Recipes for Everybody

A Complete Collection of Meat Recipes to Start Your
Plant Based Diet and Boost Your Taste

Tanya Lang

no circumstances is the author responsible for any losses, direct or indirect, which are incurred as a result of the use of information contained within this document, including, but not limited to, — errors, omissions, or inaccuracies.

TABLE OF CONTENT

Eggplant, Onion, and Tomato Stew

Preparation Time: 5 minutes | Cooking Time: 5 minutes | Servings: 4

Ingredients:

- 3 1/2 cups cubed eggplant
- 1 cup diced white onion
- 2 cups diced tomatoes
- 1 teaspoon ground cumin
- 1/8 teaspoon ground cayenne pepper
- 1 teaspoon salt
- 1 cup tomato sauce
- 1/2 cup water

Directions:

• Switch on the instant pot, place all the ingredients in it, stir until mixed, and seal the pot. • Press the _manual' button and cook for 5 minutes at a high-pressure setting until cooked. • When done, do quick pressure release, open the instant pot, and stir the stew. • Serve straight away.

Nutrition:

- Calories: 88 Cal Fat: 1 g Carbs: 21 g Protein: 3 g Fiber: 6 g

White Bean Stew

- Preparation Time: 5 minutes | Cooking Time: 10 hours and 10 minutes | Servings: 10

Ingredients:

- 2 cups chopped spinach
- 28 ounces diced tomatoes
- 2 pounds white beans, dried
- 2 cups chopped chard
- 2 large carrots, peeled, diced
- 2 cups chopped kale
- 3 large celery stalks, diced
- 1 medium white onion, peeled, diced
- 1 ½ teaspoon minced garlic
- 2 tablespoons salt
- 1 teaspoon dried rosemary
- ½ teaspoon Ground black pepper, to taste
- 1 teaspoon dried thyme
- 1 teaspoon dried oregano
- 1 bay leaf
- 10 cups water

Directions:

• Switch on the slow cooker, add all the ingredients in it, except for kale, chard, and spinach and stir until combined.

• Shut the cooker with a lid and cook for 10 hours at a low heat setting until thoroughly cooked.

• When done, stir in kale, chard, and spinach, and cook for 10 minutes until leaves wilt.

• Serve straight away.

Nutrition:

• Calories: 109 Cal Fat: 2.4 g Carbs: 17.8 g Protein: 5.3 g Fiber: 6 g

Brussel Sprouts Stew

- Preparation Time: 10 minutes | Cooking Time: 55 minutes | Servings: 4

Ingredients:

- 35 ounces Brussels sprouts
- 5 medium potato, peeled, chopped
- 1 medium onion, peeled, chopped
- 2 carrot, peeled, cubed
- 2 teaspoon smoked paprika
- 1/8 teaspoon ground black pepper
- 1/8 teaspoon salt
- 3 tablespoons caraway seeds
- 1/2 teaspoon red chili powder
- 1 tablespoon nutmeg
- 1 tablespoon olive oil
- 4 ½ cups hot vegetable stock

Directions:

- Take a large pot, place it over medium-high heat, add oil, and when hot, add onion and cook for 1 minute.
- Then add carrot and potato, cook for 2 minutes, then add Brussel sprouts and cook for 5 minutes.

• Stir in all the spices, pour in vegetable stock, bring the mixture to boil, switch heat to medium-low and simmer for 45 minutes until cooked and stew reaches the desired thickness.

• Serve straight away.

Nutrition:

• Calories: 156 Cal Fat: 3 g Carbs: 22 g Protein: 12 g Fiber: 5.1100 g

Vegetarian Gumbo

- Preparation Time: 10 minutes | Cooking Time: 45 minutes | Servings: 4

Ingredients:

- 1 1/2 cups diced zucchini
- 16-ounces cooked red beans
- 4 cups sliced okra
- 1 1/2 cups diced green pepper
- 1 1/2 cups chopped white onion
- 1 1/2 cups diced red bell pepper
- 8 cremini mushrooms, quartered
- 1 cup sliced celery
- 3 teaspoons minced garlic
- 1 medium tomato, chopped
- 1 teaspoon red pepper flakes
- 1 teaspoon dried thyme
- 3 tablespoons all-purpose flour
- 1 tablespoon smoked paprika
- 1 teaspoon dried oregano
- 1/4 teaspoon nutmeg
- 1 teaspoon soy sauce
- 1 1/2 teaspoons liquid smoke
- 2 tablespoons mustard

- 1 tablespoon apple cider vinegar
- 1 tablespoon Worcestershire sauce, vegetarian
- 1/2 teaspoon hot sauce
- 3 tablespoons olive oil
- 4 cups vegetable stock
- 1/2 cups sliced green onion
- 4 cups cooked jasmine rice

Directions:

- Take a Dutch oven, place it over medium heat, add oil and flour and cook for 5 minutes until fragrant.
- Switch heat to the medium low level, and continue cooking for 20 minutes until the roux becomes dark brown, whisking constantly.
- Meanwhile, place the tomato in a food processor, add garlic and onion along with remaining ingredients, except for stock, zucchini, celery, mushroom, green and red bell pepper, and pulse for 2 minutes until smooth.
- Pour the mixture into the pan, return pan over medium-high heat, stir until mixed, and cook for 5 minutes until all the liquid has evaporated.
- Stir in stock, bring it to simmer, then add

remaining vegetables and simmer for 20 minutes until tender.

• Garnish gumbo with green onions and serve with rice.

Nutrition:

• Calories: 160 Cal Fat: 7.3 g Carbs: 20 g Protein: 7 g Fiber: 5.7 g

Black Bean and Quinoa Stew

Preparation Time: 10 minutes | Cooking Time: 6 hours | Servings: 6

Ingredients:

- 1 pound black beans, dried, soaked overnight
- 3/4 cup quinoa, uncooked
- 1 medium red bell pepper, cored, chopped
- 1 medium red onion, peeled, diced
- 1 medium green bell pepper, cored, chopped
- 28-ounce diced tomatoes
- 2 dried chipotle peppers
- 1 ½ teaspoon minced garlic
- 2/3 teaspoon sea salt
- 2 teaspoons red chili powder
- 1/3 teaspoon ground black pepper
- 1 teaspoon coriander powder
- 1 dried cinnamon stick

- 1/4 cup cilantro
- 7 cups of water

Directions:

- Switch on the slow cooker, add all the ingredients in it, except for salt, and stir until mixed. • Shut the cooker with a lid and cook for 6 hours at a high heat setting until cooked. • When done, stir salt into the stew until mixed, remove cinnamon sticks and serve.

Nutrition:

- Calories: 308 Cal Fat: 2 g Carbs: 70 g Protein: 23 g Fiber: 32 g

Root Vegetable Stew

• Preparation Time: 10 minutes | Cooking Time: 8 hours and 10 minutes | Servings: 6

Ingredients:

- 2 cups chopped kale
- 1 large white onion, peeled, chopped
- 1 pound parsnips, peeled, chopped
- 1 pound potatoes, peeled, chopped
- 2 celery ribs, chopped
- 1 pound butternut squash, peeled, deseeded, chopped
- 1 pound carrots, peeled, chopped
- 3 teaspoons minced garlic
- 1 pound sweet potatoes, peeled, chopped
- 1 bay leaf
- 1 teaspoon ground black pepper
- 1/2 teaspoon sea salt
- 1 tablespoon chopped sage
- 3 cups vegetable broth

Directions:

• Switch on the slow cooker, add all the ingredients in it, except for the kale, and stir until mixed.

- Shut the cooker with a lid and cook for 8 hours at a low heat setting until cooked.
- When done, add kale into the stew, stir until mixed, and cook for 10 minutes until leaves have wilted.
- Serve straight away.

Nutrition:
- Calories: 120 Cal Fat: 1 g Carbs: 28 g Protein: 4 g Fiber: 6 g

Portobello Mushroom Stew

Preparation Time: 10 minutes | Cooking Time: 8 hours | Servings: 4

Ingredients:

- 8 cups vegetable broth
- 1 cup dried wild mushrooms
- 1 cup dried chickpeas
- 3 cups chopped potato
- 2 cups chopped carrots
- 1 cup corn kernels
- 2 cups diced white onions
- 1 tablespoon minced parsley
- 3 cups chopped zucchini
- 1 tablespoon minced rosemary
- 1 1/2 teaspoon ground black pepper
- 1 teaspoon dried sage
- 2/3 teaspoon salt
- 1 teaspoon dried oregano
- 3 tablespoons soy sauce
- 1 1/2 teaspoons liquid smoke
- 8 ounces tomato paste

Directions:

• Switch on the slow cooker, add all the ingredients in it, and stir until mixed. • Shut the cooker with a lid and cook for 10 hours at a high heat setting until cooked. • Serve straight away.

Nutrition:

• Calories: 447 Cal Fat: 36 g Carbs: 24 g Protein: 11 g Fiber: 2 g

Fresh Bean Soup

• Preparation Time: 05 minutes | Cooking Time: 15 minutes | Servings: 4

Ingredients:

- 2 tablespoons olive oil
- 2 medium onions, finely chopped
- 2 cups of water
- 3 cups fresh shelled green beans
- Salt and pepper to taste

Directions:

• Heat the olive oil in a heavy-bottomed saucepan over medium heat. Cook the onions until soft and translucent, about 3 minutes. Pour in the water and beans, season to taste with salt and pepper. Increase the heat to medium-high, bring to a boil, then reduce heat to low, cover, and simmer until the peas are tender, 12 to 18 minutes.

• Puree the peas in a blender or food processor in batches. Strain back into the saucepan. Season to taste with salt and pepper before serving.

Nutrition:

- Calories 111, Total Fat 7.2g, Saturated Fat 1g, Cholesterol 0mg, Sodium 8mg, Total Carbohydrate 10.4g, Dietary Fiber 3g, Total Sugars 4.4g, Protein 2.6g, Calcium 25mg, Iron 1mg, Potassium 170mg, Phosphorus 104mg

Macaroni Soup

• Preparation Time: 15 minutes | Cooking Time: 55 minutes | Servings: 4

Ingredients:

- 2 tablespoons olive oil
- 2 large cloves garlic, minced
- 1 large onion finely chopped
- 1 cup of water
- 1/4 teaspoon Italian seasoning 1 tablespoon chopped fresh parsley
- 1/4 teaspoon garlic powder
- Black pepper to taste
- 1 cup macaroni

Directions:

• Heat the olive oil in a soup pot over medium-low heat. Stir in the minced garlic and onion; cook and stir until soft, about 5 minutes. Turn heat to medium; stir in water, Italian seasoning, parsley, garlic powder, and pepper. Bring to a simmer. Cook for 40 minutes with the lid slightly ajar.

• Stir macaroni into soup; cook at a strong simmer until macaroni is tender, about 12 minutes.

Nutrition:

- Calories 116, Total Fat 5.1g, Saturated Fat 0.7g, Cholesterol 0mg, Sodium 4mg, Total Carbohydrate 14.7g, Dietary Fiber 1.7g, Total Sugars 1.9g, Protein 3.2g, Calcium 13mg, Iron 1mg, Potassium 100mg, Phosphorus 105 mg

Carrot, cauliflower, and Cabbage Soup

• Preparation Time: 30 minutes | Cooking Time: 20 minutes | Servings: 4

Ingredients:

- 4 large carrots, thinly sliced
- 1 cup cauliflower, thinly sliced
- 1 large onion, thinly sliced
- 1/4 medium head green cabbage, thinly sliced
- 2 cloves garlic, smashed
- 6 cups of water
- 1 tablespoon olive oil
- 1/4 teaspoon dried thyme
- 1/4 teaspoon dried basil
- 1 teaspoon dried parsley
- 1/8 teaspoon salt
- Ground black pepper to taste

Directions:

• Combine the carrots, cauliflower, onion, cabbage, garlic, water, olive oil, thyme, basil, parsley, salt, and pepper in a pot over medium-high heat; bring to a simmer and cook until the carrots are tender for about 20 minutes. Transfer to a blender in small batches and blend until smooth.

Nutrition:

- Calories 57, Total Fat 2.4g, Saturated Fat 0.3g, Cholesterol 0mg, Sodium 98mg, Total Carbohydrate 8.5g, Dietary Fiber 2.3g, Total Sugars 4g, Protein 1.1g, Calcium 37mg, Iron 0mg, Potassium 249mg, Phosphorus 150 mg

Carrot Soup

- Preparation Time: 15 minutes | Cooking Time: 20 minutes | Servings: 4

Ingredients:

- 3 cups carrots, chopped
- 6 cups of water
- 3 cloves garlic, chopped
- 2 tablespoons dried dill weed
- 1/4 pound olive oil
- 1/8 teaspoons salt

Directions:

- In a medium-sized pot, over high heat, combine the water, carrots, garlic, dill weed, salt, and olive oil. Bring to a boil, reduce heat and simmer for 30 minutes or until carrots are soft. • In a blender, puree the soup, return to the pot and simmer for an additional 30 to 45 minutes. Season with additional dill or garlic if needed.

Nutrition:

- Calories 169, Total Fat 17.7g, Saturated Fat 2.5g, Cholesterol 0mg, Sodium 81mg,

Total Carbohydrate 4.1g, Dietary Fiber
0.9g, Total Sugars 1.5g, Protein 0.6g,
Calcium 38mg, Iron 1mg, Potassium

140mg, Phosphorus 90 mg

Vegetable Barley Soup

Preparation Time: 5 minutes | Cooking Time: 15 minutes | Servings: 8

Ingredients:

- 1 cup barley
- 14.5 ounces diced tomatoes with juice
- 2 large carrots, chopped
- 15 ounces cooked chickpeas
- 2 stalks celery, chopped
- 1 zucchini, chopped
- 1 medium white onion, peeled, chopped
- 1/2 teaspoon ground black pepper
- 1 teaspoon garlic powder
- 1 teaspoon curry powder
- 1 teaspoon salt
- 1 teaspoon paprika
- 1 teaspoon white sugar
- 1 teaspoon dried parsley
- 1 teaspoon Worcestershire sauce
- 3 bay leaves
- 2 quarts vegetable broth

Directions:

- Place all the ingredients in a pot, stir until mixed, place it over medium-high heat and bring the mixture to a boil.
- Switch heat to medium level, simmer the soup for 90 minutes until cooked, and when done, remove bay leaf from it.
- Serve straight away.

Nutrition:
- Calories: 188 Cal Fat: 1.6 g Carbs: 37 g Protein: 7 g Fiber: 8.4 g

Mushroom, Lentil, and Barley Stew

Preparation Time: 10 minutes | Cooking Time: 6 hours | Servings: 8

Ingredients:

- 3/4 cup pearl barley
- 2 cups sliced button mushrooms
- 3/4 cup dry lentils
- 1 ounce dried shiitake mushrooms
- 2 teaspoons minced garlic
- 1/4 cup dried onion flakes
- 2 teaspoons ground black pepper
- 1 teaspoon dried basil
- 2 ½ teaspoons salt
- 2 teaspoons dried savory
- 3 bay leaves
- 2 quarts vegetable broth

Directions:

• Switch on the slow cooker, place all the ingredients in it, and stir until combined. • Shut with lid and cook the stew for 6 hours at a high heat setting until cooked. • Serve straight away.

Nutrition:

• Calories: 213 Cal Fat: 1.2 g Carbs: 44 g Protein: 8.4 g Fiber: 9 g

Tomato Barley Soup

- Preparation Time: 10 minutes | Cooking Time: 40 minutes | Servings: 6

Ingredients:

- 1/4 cup barley
- 1 cup chopped celery
- 14.5 ounces peeled and diced tomatoes
- 1 cup chopped white onions
- 2 tomatoes, diced
- 1 cup chopped carrots
- 2 teaspoons minced garlic
- 1/8 teaspoon ground black pepper
- 1 teaspoon salt
- 2 tablespoons olive oil
- 2 1/2 cups water
- 10.75 ounces chicken broth

Directions:

• Take a large saucepan, place it over medium heat, add onion, carrot, and celery, stir in garlic and cook for 10 minutes until tender.

• Then add remaining ingredients, stir until combined, and bring the mixture to a boil.

- Switch heat to the level, simmer the soup for 40 minutes and then serve straight away.

Nutrition:
- Calories: 129 Cal Fat: 5.5 g Carbs: 15.3 g Protein: 4.6 g Fiber: 3.7 g

Sweet Potato, Kale, and Peanut Stew

- Preparation Time: 10 minutes | Cooking Time: 45 minutes | Servings: 3

Ingredients:

- 1/4 cup red lentils
- 2 medium sweet potatoes, peeled, cubed
- 1 medium white onion, peeled, diced
- 1 cup kale, chopped
- 2 tomatoes, diced
- 1/4 cup chopped green onion
- 1 teaspoon minced garlic
- 1 inch of ginger, grated
- 2 tablespoons toasted peanuts
- ¼ teaspoon ground black pepper
- 1 teaspoon ground cumin
- 1/2 teaspoon turmeric
- 1/8 teaspoon cayenne pepper
- 1 tablespoon peanut butter
- 1 1/2 cups vegetable broth
- 2 teaspoons coconut oil

Directions:

• Take a medium pot, place it on medium heat, add oil and when it melts, add onions and cook for 5 minutes.

• Then stir in ginger and garlic, cook for 2 minutes until fragrant, add lentils and potatoes along with all the spices, and stir until mixed.

• Stir in tomatoes, pour in the broth, bring the mixture to boil, then switch heat to the low level and simmer for 30 minutes until cooked.

• Then stir in peanut butter until incorporated and then puree by using an immersion blender until half-pureed.

• Return stew over low heat, stir in kale, cook for 5 minutes until its leaves wilts, and then season with black pepper and salt.

• Garnish the stew with peanuts and green onions and then serve.

Nutrition:

• Calories: 401 Cal Fat: 6.7 g Carbs: 77.3 g Protein: 10.8 g Fiber: 16 g

Lentil Stew

• Preparation Time: 35 minutes | Cooking Time: 30-120 minutes | Servings: 4

Ingredients:
- 1 cup red lentils, soaked
- 1 medium-sized onion, peeled and finely chopped
- ½ cup sweet carrot puree
- 1 tbsp all-purpose flour
- ½ tsp freshly ground black pepper
- ½ tsp cumin, ground
- ½ tsp salt
- 2 tbsp olive oil

Directions:
- Soak the lentils overnight.
- Rinse well the lentils under cold running water using a large colander. Drain well and set

aside.

• Plug your instant pot and grease the stainless steel insert with olive oil. Press the —Sautell button and heat it. Add onions and flour. Cook for 10 minutes, stirring constantly. • Now, add the remaining ingredients and pour in about 4 cups of water. Close the lid and set

the release steam handle. Press the ─Manual‖ button and cook for 30 minutes on high

pressure.

• Press the ─Cancel‖ button and release the steam handle. Turn off the pot and set it aside to

chill for a while before serving.

• Optionally, sprinkle with cayenne pepper and parsley.

Nutrition:

• Calories: 140 Cal Fat: 0.9 g Carbs: 27.1 g Protein: 6.3 g Fiber: 6.2 g

Ginger Stew

• Preparation Time: 35 minutes | Cooking Time: 30-120 minutes | Servings: 4

Ingredients:

- 2 cups green peas
- 1 large onion, chopped
- 4 cloves of garlic, finely chopped
- 3 ½ oz of olives, pitted
- 1 tbsp of ginger, ground
- 1 tbsp of turmeric, ground
- 1 tbsp of salt
- 4 cups of vegetable stock
- 3 tbsp olive oil

Directions:

• Rinse well the green peas using a large colander. Drain and set aside.

• Plug your instant pot and press the —Sautell button. Heat the olive oil in the stainless steel

insert and add onions and garlic. Stir-fry for 2-3 minutes, or until translucent. • Now, add the

remaining ingredients and close the lid. Set the steam release handle and press
the —Stew‖ button.

• When you hear the cooker's end signal, perform a quick release.

• Open the pot and serve immediately.

Nutrition:

• Calories: 140 Cal Fat: 0.9 g Carbs: 27.1 g Protein: 6.3 g Fiber: 6.2 g

Ziti Mushroom Stew

- Preparation Time: 6 minutes | Cooking Time: 30-120 minutes | Servings: 4 Ingredients:
  - 1bell pepper, seeded and minced
  - 1onion, minced
  - 1 (14-ounce can crushed tomatoes
  - 4garlic cloves, minced
  - 2tablespoons tomato paste
  - ½cup dry red wine
  - 8ounces white mushrooms, coarsely chopped
  - 1cup hot water
  - 8ounces uncooked ziti
  - 1teaspoon dried basil
  - Salt and black pepper
  - 2teaspoons minced fresh oregano
  - 1teaspoon natural sugar
  - 2tablespoons chopped parsley

Directions:

- Add the ziti, mushroom, red wine, tomato paste in an instant pot.

- Add the sugar, herbs, spices, hot water, and the rest of the ingredients.

- Mix well and cook for 5 minutes with the lid on.
- Serve hot.

Nutrition:
- Calories:680, Total Fat:71.8g, Saturated Fat:20.9g, Total Carbs:10g, Dietary Fiber:7g, Sugar:2g, Protein:3g, Sodium:525mg

Spiced Red Lentil Vegetable Stew

• Preparation Time: 25 minutes | Cooking Time: 30 minutes | Servings: 2

Ingredients:
- 1 1/2 tablespoon olive oil
- ½ zucchini, thinly sliced
- 1 small onion, diced
- 1 leek, diced
- ½ teaspoon garlic powder
- ¼ teaspoon salt
- ¼ teaspoon turmeric powder
- ¼ teaspoon paprika
- 2 cups vegetable broth
- ½ cup diced tomatoes
- ½ cup chickpeas drained and rinsed
- ½ cup sweet potatoes, quartered
- ½ cup dried red lentils
- ½ tablespoon fresh basil, chopped
- ½ cup goat cheese, shredded (optional

Directions:

• Set Instant Pot to Sauté and heat olive oil; cook zucchini, onions, leeks, and garlic powder, stirring occasionally until softened, about 6 minutes. Add salt, turmeric powder, and paprika; cook, stirring, for 1 minute.

• Stir in vegetable broth, tomatoes, chickpeas, sweet potatoes, red lentils, and water; Close the steam valve, press the Manual button, select High pressure, then press the + button to increase the time to 20 minutes.

• Once the pressure has been released, open the steam valve, and then remove the lid. Stir in basil and goat cheese.

Nutrition:

• Calories 569, Total Fat 14. 9g, Saturated Fat 3. 6g, Cholesterol 7mg, Sodium 1113mg, Total Carbohydrate 79. 9g, Dietary Fiber 27. 1g, Total Sugars 13. 1g, Protein 31. 9g

Pinto Bean Stew with Cauliflower

- Preparation Time: 10 minutes | Cooking Time: 25 minutes | Servings: 2

Ingredients:

- 1 cup of water
- 1 teaspoon salt
- ¼ cup pinto beans
- 2 tablespoons coconut oil
- ½ small onion chopped
- 1 small zucchini chopped
- ½ teaspoon garlic powder
- 1 bay leaf
- 1 1/2 cups low sodium vegetable stock
- ½ cup steamed cauliflower
- ¼ cup grated mozzarella
- 1 tablespoon chopped fresh cilantro

Directions:

- In a large bowl, dissolve 1 tablespoon of salt in the water. Add the pinto beans and soak at room temperature for 8 to 24 hours. Drain and rinse.

• Select Sauté and adjust to Normal or Medium heat. Add the coconut oil to the Instant Pot and heat until shimmering. Add the onion and zucchini, and sprinkle with salt. Cook, stirring often until the onion pieces separate and soften. Add the garlic powder and cook for about 1 minute, or until fragrant. Add the drained pinto beans, remaining ¼ teaspoon of salt, bay leaf, and vegetable stock.

• Lock the lid into place. Select Pressure Cook or Manual, and adjust the pressure to High and the time to 15 minutes. After cooking, let the pressure release naturally for 10 minutes, then quickly release any remaining pressure.

• Unlock the lid. Stir in the cauliflower and bring to a simmer to heat it through and thicken the sauce slightly. Taste the beans and adjust the seasoning. Ladle into bowls and sprinkle with the mozzarella cheese and cilantro.

Nutrition:

• Calories 245, Total Fat 16. 2g, Saturated Fat 13. 7g, Cholesterol 2mg, Sodium 1745mg, Total Carbohydrate 22. 4g, Dietary Fiber 5. 6g, Total Sugars 4. 5g, Protein 7. 7g

Pumpkin Stew

- Preparation Time: 10 minutes | Cooking Time: 15 minutes | Servings: 2

Ingredients:
- 1 cup vegetable broth
- 1 1/2 cups pumpkin cut into small cubes
- 1 cup kidney beans cooked, rinsed, and drained
- 1 cup onion chopped
- ½ cup green peas
- 1 teaspoon garlic powder
- ½ cup diced tomatoes
- 1 teaspoon red chili
- ¼ teaspoon ground cumin

Directions:
- Place all the ingredients in the inner pot. Cover with a lid, turn the lid clockwise to lock into place. Align the pointed end of the steam release handle to point to —Sealing‖. Press "Manual", use the [-] button to adjust cooking time to 5 minutes.
- When cooking time is complete, press "Keep Warm/Cancel" once to Cancel the keep warm mode

then wait 10 minutes for the pressure to go down.

• Slide the steam release handle to the —Venting‖ position to release the remaining pressure until the float valve drops down.

• Remove the lid. Allow to cool for 10 minutes before serving. Enjoy!

Nutrition:

• Calories245, Total Fat 2. 4g, Saturated Fat 0. 4g, Cholesterol 0mg, Sodium 805mg, Total Carbohydrate 43. 2g, Dietary Fiber 13. 6g, Total Sugars 11. 4g, Protein 14. 5g

Cauliflower and Bean Stew

- Preparation Time: 10 minutes | Cooking Time: 10 minutes | Servings: 2

Ingredients:

- 1 cup cauliflower cut into 1-inch pieces
- 1 cup chickpea rinsed and drained
- 1 cup black beans, rinsed and drained
- ½ cup crushed tomatoes preferably fire-roasted
- 1 small onion chopped
- ¼ cup vegetable broth
- 1 orange juice
- 1 canned chipotle pepper in adobo sauce minced
- 1 teaspoon salt
- 1 teaspoon ground cumin
- 1 bay leaf
- Fresh cilantro sprigs

Directions:

- Combine cauliflower, chickpea, black beans, tomatoes, onions, broth, orange juice, chipotle pepper, salt, cumin, and bay leaf in Instant Pot; mix well.
- Secure lid and move pressure release valve to

sealing position. Press Manual or Pressure Cook; cook at High pressure 6 minutes.

• When cooking is complete, use Natural-release for 5 minutes, then release remaining pressure.

• Press Sauté; cook 3 to 5 minutes or until the stew thickens slightly, stirring frequently. Remove and discard bay leaf. Garnish with cilantro.

Nutrition:

• Calories 614, Total Fat 4. 6g, Saturated Fat 0. 9g, Cholesterol 0mg, Sodium 1816mg, Total Carbohydrate 115. 3g, Dietary Fiber 24. 8g, Total Sugars 12g, Protein 32. 9g

Cabbage Soup

- Preparation Time: 10 minutes | Cooking Time: 20 minutes | Servings: 2

Ingredients:

- 1 head cabbage
- ½ tablespoon dried basil
- 2 Oz Cheddar cheese chunks
- ½ tablespoon coconut cream
- ½ teaspoon garlic powder
- Salt to taste

Directions:

- Add all ingredients to the blender pitcher and lock the lid.
- Select the —Soup‖ setting for 20:00 minutes.
- Garnish with shredded cheddar cheese and serve.

Nutrition:

- Calories 213, Total Fat 10. 5g, Saturated Fat 6. 8g, Cholesterol 29mg, Sodium 316mg, Total Carbohydrate 21. 8g, Dietary Fiber 9. 1g, Total Sugars 11. 9g, Protein 11. 8g

Vegetable Stew

• Preparation Time: 15 minutes | Cooking Time: 20 minutes | Servings: 2

Ingredients:
- 1 small onion, minced
- 1 teaspoon garlic powder
- 1 leek, minced
- ½ zucchini, minced
- 1/4 cup vegetable broth
- 2 oz. button mushrooms, sliced
- 1 teaspoon dried basil
- ½ teaspoon Italian seasoning
- 1/2 teaspoon salt
- 1/4 teaspoon ground pepper
- 2 tomatoes, chopped
- 1 medium parsnip, chopped
- ½ yum, chopped
- ¼ tablespoon balsamic vinegar
- 1 tablespoon cornstarch
- ¼ cup green beans
- Enough water

Directions:

• Add onion and mushrooms to the Instant Pot. Press the Sauté button and sauté until mushrooms have released their liquid and shrunk in size, about 8 minutes. Stir every couple of minutes.

• Add garlic powder and sauté for 2 more minutes. Add salt, basil, pepper. Stir.

• Press Cancel to stop Sauté function. Lock lid in place.

• Add the remaining ingredients to the pot with broth. Press Manual and adjust the time to 10 minutes of pressure cooking.

• Meanwhile add water and cornstarch and make a mixer.

• When the time has lapsed, quickly release the pressure from the Instant Pot. Remove the lid from you.

• Add a cornstarch mixer into the pot and make a thick soup.

• Carefully transfer soup into a bowl, serve, and enjoy.

Nutrition:

• Calories 158, Total Fat 1. 2g, Saturated Fat 0. 2g,

Cholesterol 1mg, Sodium 714mg, Total
Carbohydrate 35. 1g, Dietary Fiber 6. 4g, Total
Sugars 11. 1g, Protein 5. 5g

Cauliflower Soup

Preparation Time: 10 minutes | Cooking Time: 5 minutes | Servings: 2

Ingredients:

- 5 cups vegetable broth or water
- 1 medium onion chopped
- 1 - 2 stalks leek thinly sliced
- 2 cloves garlic crushed
- 1 lb. cauliflower cut in big chunks
- 1 teaspoon salt
- 1/2 teaspoon pepper
- 1 teaspoon fresh basil
- 1/4 cup almond flour
- 2/3 cup water
- 1 cup grated goat cheese
- 1/2 cup milk
- Salt and pepper to taste

Directions:

• Add the first 8 ingredients (including basil) to the Instant Pot and lock lid. Make sure the valve is set to Sealing and press Pressure Cooker (or Manual). Set the time with the + /button for 5 minutes.

- While cooking, stir in flour and water until smooth. When the IP beeps, flip the valve from Sealing to Venting and when the pin drops, press Cancel and remove the lid.
- Press the Sauté button and cook again, stirring frequently. Whisk the flour-water mixture and add about half of it to the soup.
- Use a hand blender to puree the soup. Or use a blender or food processor and put it back in the pan.
- Press Cancel and add the cheese. Stir until melted. Do not cook after the cheese has gone in. Add the milk, salt, and pepper to your taste. Serve with a pinch of grated cheese.

Nutrition:
- Calories 202, Total Fat 8. 4g, Saturated Fat 4. 4g, Cholesterol 20mg, Sodium 1345mg, Total Carbohydrate 23. 2g, Dietary Fiber 7. 8g, Total Sugars 11. 3g, Protein 12. 6g

Pumpkin Soup

- Preparation Time: 10 minutes | Cooking Time: 20 minutes | Servings: 2

Ingredients:

- 1 lb pumpkin peeled and seeded 1/2-1inch cubes
- 1 cup vegetable broth or water
- 1 teaspoon dried rosemary
- 1/4 teaspoon grated cinnamon
- 1/2 teaspoon salt
- 1 cup of coconut milk
- 2 tablespoons butter
- 1 tablespoon almond flour

Directions:

- Mix the pumpkin cubes, broth, rosemary, cinnamon, and salt in an Instant Pot. Lock the lid onto the pot.
- Press Soup/Broth, Pressure Cooker, or Manual on High Pressure for 5 minutes with the Keep Warm setting off. The valve must be closed.
- Use the Quick-release mode to return the pot pressure to normal. Unlock the lid and open the pot. Add coconut milk.

- Use an immersion blender to puree the soup right in the pot. Or work in halves to puree the soup in a covered blender. If necessary, pour all the soup back into the pan.
- Press the Sauté button and set it for Low, 250°F. Set the timer for 5 minutes.
- Bring the soup to a simmer, stirring often. In the meantime, place the butter in a small bowl or measuring container and place it in the microwave in 5-second increments. Use a fork to mix the flour and make a thin paste.
- When the soup is boiling, Whisk the butter mixture in the pan. Continue whisking until the soup is a bit thick, about 1 minute. Turn off the Sauté function and allow it to cool for a few minutes before serving.

Nutrition:
- Calories 415, Total Fat 41g, Saturated Fat 32. 9g, Cholesterol 31mg, Sodium 1064mg, Total Carbohydrate 11. 5g, Dietary Fiber 3. 3g, Total Sugars 5. 2g, Protein 5. 9g

Almond Broccoli Soup

• Preparation Time: 05 minutes | Cooking Time: 20 minutes | Servings: 2

Ingredients:

- 1/2 cup roasted almond divided
- 2 1/2 cups vegetable broth divided
- ½ tablespoon fresh basil leaves chopped
- ½ tablespoon fresh oregano leaves chopped
- 1 teaspoon garlic powder
- 15 oz can chickpeas drained and rinsed
- 1 small onion roughly chopped
- 1 small head broccoli cut into florets

Directions:

- Add an almond to the blender pitcher and lock the lid.
- Touch Pulse, then touch Start.
- When the Pulse program is complete, scrape down the sides and bottom of the Pitcher. • Add 1/2 cup broth and lock the lid.
- Touch Pulse, then Start.

- When the Pulse program is complete, add the remaining broth, herbs, garlic powder,

chickpeas, onion, and broccoli--in that order-- and lock the lid.

- Touch Soup two times and use +/- to set the time to 14 minutes, then touch Start. • Adjust seasonings and Serve.

Nutrition:

- Calories192, Total Fat 9. 7g, Saturated Fat 0. 7g, Cholesterol 0mg, Sodium 450mg, Total Carbohydrate 20. 4g, Dietary Fiber 4g, Total Sugars 6. 4g, Protein 7. 8g

Jackfruit Stew

- Preparation Time: 10 minutes | Cooking Time: 25 minutes | Servings: 2

Ingredients:
- 1 large onion chopped
- 3 cloves garlic minced
- 1 1/2 cup vegetable broth
- 1 teaspoon salt
- 1/2 teaspoon pepper
- 1 cup jackfruit
- 1 sweet potato cut into 1-inch pieces
- 1 carrot cut into 1-inch pieces
- ½ cup frozen peas
- 1 tablespoon cornstarch
- 3 tablespoons water
- 2 tablespoons chopped fresh parsley

Directions:

- Mix the first six ingredients, including the jackfruit, in the Instant Pot. Lock lid in place and turn the valve to Sealing. Press the Pressure Cooker button and set the cooking time for 20 minutes at High Pressure.

- During cooking, cut sweet potatoes and carrots with or without peel into 1-inch pieces. Make a mixture by stirring the corn-starch in the water until smooth.
- When the Instant Pot beeps, let it go for 10 minutes. Release the remaining pressure naturally and open the pot when the pin drops.
- Add the sweet potatoes and carrots (not the peas) and gently squeeze them into the liquid. Lock lid and press hit pressure (or Manual). Set the cooking time to 4 minutes. When it's done, take a quick release (pin drop), open the pot.
- Tap Cancel then Sauté. Stir in the corn-starch and add about half of the mortar as the stew cooks. Boil to thicken it, and if you want thicker, add more.
- Press Cancel and add frozen peas. The heat of the stew is enough to cook them without turning them into mush. Add salt and pepper if necessary. Add the parsley if you use it,

Nutrition:
- Calories 267, Total Fat 1. 8g, Saturated Fat 0. 4g, Cholesterol 0mg, Sodium 1786mg, Total Carbohydrate 56g, Dietary Fiber 8. 1g, Total Sugars

7. 5g, Protein 10g

Ginger & Turmeric Carrot Soup

• Preparation Time: 10 minutes | Cooking Time: 25 minutes | Servings: 2

Ingredients:
- ½ tablespoon butter
- 1 onion and sliced
- 1 1/2 cups chopped carrots
- ½ cup chopped pumpkin
- ¼ cup tomato, chopped
- 1 teaspoon garlic powder
- 1 tablespoon grated ginger
- 1 tablespoon turmeric powder
- Salt & pepper to taste
- 3 cups vegetable broth
- 1 cup of coconut milk

Directions:
- Set on Sauté mode and pour in the butter.
- Add in the diced onion, carrots, and mix until combined.
- Sauté for about 5 minutes or until the vegetables

become soft.

- Stir in the garlic powder, ginger turmeric powder, salt, and pepper.
- Add in the pumpkin, tomatoes, broth, coconut milk, and stir to combine.
- Lock the lid in place and close the steam vent.
- Set on Manual or Pressure Cooker on High Pressure for 4 minutes.
- Allow the Instant Pot to Natural-release for 5 minutes once the timer goes off. • Remove the lid and stir to combine.
- Enjoy!

Nutrition:

- Calories 435, Total Fat 34. 3g, Saturated Fat 28g, Cholesterol 8mg, Sodium 1228mg, Total Carbohydrate 25. 1g, Dietary Fiber 7. 4g, Total Sugars 11. 2g, Protein 12. 2g

Coconut Tofu Soup

- Preparation Time: 10 minutes | Cooking Time: 10 minutes | Servings: 2

Ingredients:

- 2 cups vegetable broth or water
- 1/2 pound tofu
- ½ cup full fat coconut milk
- 1 tablespoon ginger
- 2 whole red chills
- ½ tablespoon lemon zest
- 1 teaspoon maple syrup
- 1/2 teaspoon salt
- 1/4 cup fresh lime juice from 2 or 3 limes
- Chopped fresh parsley for garnish
- Lime wedges for serving

Directions:

- In the Instant Pot, combine the broth, tofu, half the coconut milk, the ginger, chills (if using), lemon zest, maple syrup, and salt.
- Lock lid on the Instant Pot. Close the Pressure-release valve. Select Manual or Pressure Cooker and set the pot at Low Pressure for 1 minute. At the end

of the cooking time, quickly release the pressure.

• Stir in the remaining coconut milk, and lime juice.

• Divide the soup among two serving bowls.
Garnish with parsley and serve with lime wedges
alongside for squeezing.

Nutrition:

• Calories 238, Total Fat 19. 2g, Saturated Fat 13.
7g, Cholesterol 0mg, Sodium 31mg, Total
Carbohydrate 10. 3g, Dietary Fiber 2. 9g, Total
Sugars 5g, Protein 11g

Millet Soup

- Preparation Time: 10 minutes | Cooking Time: 30 minutes | Servings: 2

Ingredients:
- ½ tablespoon butter
- 1/4 cup onion
- ½ cup chopped parsnips
- ½ cup sliced leeks,
- 1 teaspoon garlic powder
- ½ tablespoon lemon zest
- Pinch of salt & pepper
- ¼ cup millet
- 2 cups vegetable broth
- ½ cup of soy milk
- 1/8 cup lemon juice
- 1 cup fresh Swiss chard

Directions:

- Heat the butter in an Instant Pot and select the Sauté function. When butter melts add the onion, parsnips, leeks, and garlic powder and sauté until soft, about 5 minutes.
- Add lemon zest, broth, and millet, salt, and

pepper, and stir to combine. Lock lid in place and turn the valve to Sealing. Press the Pressure Cooker button and set the cooking time for 20 minutes at High Pressure.

- When the Instant Pot beeps, let it go for 10 minutes. Release the remaining pressure naturally and open the pot when the pin drops.
- Once the Millet is cooked and soft, stir in the soy milk, lemon juice, and Swiss chard. Stir until Swiss chard is wilted.
- Lock lid and press hit pressure (or Manual). Set the cooking time to 4 minutes. When it's done, take a quick release (pin drop), open the Instant Pot.
- Serve immediately and enjoy! Soup can be frozen and reheated as desired.

Nutrition:
- Calories 249, Total Fat 6. 8g, Saturated Fat 2. 7g, Cholesterol 8mg, Sodium 867mg, Total Carbohydrate 35. 8g, Dietary Fiber 5. 4g, Total Sugars 7. 2g, Protein 11. 3g

White Lima beans Stew

- Preparation Time: 15 minutes | Cooking Time: 40 minutes | Servings: 2

Ingredients:

- ½ cup kale
- ½ tablespoons coconut oil
- 1 medium onion, chopped
- ½ teaspoon ginger powder
- ½ small bell pepper, seeded and finely chopped
- ½ teaspoon garlic powder
- ¼ tablespoon curry powder
- 1 medium zucchini, peeled and thinly sliced
- ¼ medium head broccoli, broken into bite-size florets
- ½ can white lima beans, rinsed
- 1 small diced tomato
- ¼ cup almond milk
- 2 cups vegetable broth or water
- Salt to taste

Directions:

- In a large bowl, add the white lima beans and soak at room temperature for 8 to 24 hours.

Drain and rinse.

- Select Sauté and adjust to Normal or Medium heat. Add the coconut oil to the inner pot of Instant Pot and heat. Add the onion and zucchini and sprinkle with 1/4 teaspoon of salt.

Cook, stirring often until the onion pieces separate and soften. Add the garlic powder and ginger powder and cook for about 1 minute, or until fragrant. Add the drained white lima beans, remaining 1/4 teaspoon of salt tomatoes, and broth.

- Lock lid in place and turn the valve to Sealing. Press the Pressure Cooker button and set the cooking time for 5 minutes at High Pressure. After cooking, let the pressure release naturally for 10 minutes, then quickly release any remaining pressure.

- Unlock the lid. Stir in the broccoli, kale bell pepper, and almond milk and bring to a simmer to heat it through and thicken the sauce slightly.

- Serve.

Nutrition:

- Calories 205, Total Fat 11. 4g, Saturated Fat 9.

4g, Cholesterol 0mg, Sodium 121mg, Total
Carbohydrate 23. 4g, Dietary Fiber 6. 3g, Total
Sugars 8. 4g, Protein 6. 3g

Lentil Soup with Spinach

• Preparation Time: 10 minutes | Cooking Time: 40 minutes | Servings: 2

Ingredients:

- ¼ cup lentils
- 4 cups water, divided
- 1 tablespoon butter
- 1 small onion, diced
- 1 small beetroot, diced
- ½ teaspoon salt, divided
- 1/8 teaspoon ground pepper
- ½ teaspoon garlic powder,
- ¼ teaspoon ground coriander
- ½ cup chopped spinach
- ½ cup small sweet potatoes, quartered

Directions:

- Wash the lentils very well and pick out any stones.
- Add lentils and water to the Instant Pot and stir well.
- Cover the Instant Pot and lock it in.
- Make sure the vent on top is set to

—Sealingǁ. Set Manual or Pressure Cooker Timer for 25

minutes.

• Once the timer reaches zero, quickly release the pressure. Keep aside.

• Then Select Sauté and adjust to medium heat. Add the butter to the Instant Pot and heat until

melted. Add the onions and beetroot, sweet potato, and sprinkle salt and pepper. Cook, stirring often until the onion softens. Add the garlic powder and ground coriander cook for about 1 minute, or until fragrant. Add water and lock the lid into place. Select Pressure Cooker or Manual, and adjust the pressure to High and the time to 5 minutes. After cooking, let the pressure release naturally for 5minutes, then quickly release any remaining pressure.

• Unlock the lid. Stir in the spinach and bring to a simmer to heat it through spinach wilt. Then add cooked lentils and adjust it tasty to add salt and pepper.

• Serve and enjoy.

Nutrition:

• Calories 211, Total Fat 6. 2g, Saturated Fat 3. 7g, Cholesterol 15mg, Sodium 689mg, Total Carbohydrate 31. 7g, Dietary Fiber 9. 4g, Total Sugars 6. 2g, Protein 8. 4g

Chickpea and Mushroom Soup

• Preparation Time: 05 minutes | Cooking Time: 30 minutes | Servings: 2

Ingredients:

- ½ tablespoon avocado oil
- 8 ounces mushrooms, sliced/chopped
- ¼ onion chopped
- ½ teaspoon garlic powder
- ½ can chickpeas, drained & rinsed
- 2 cups vegetable broth
- ½ tablespoon dried Italian seasoning
- ½ teaspoon dried basil
- Pinch of hot pepper flakes
- Salt & pepper to taste

Directions:

• Select Sauté and adjust to Normal heat. Add the avocado oil to the Instant Pot and heat. Add garlic powder and onion and cook until the onions are slightly opaque and beginning to brown. Add mushrooms, when the mushrooms start to soften, add the spices, seasonings, and the chickpeas. Season with salt and pepper. Add broth and lock the lid into place. Select Pressure Cooker or Manual, and adjust the pressure to High and the time to 20minutes. After cooking, let the pressure release naturally for 5 minutes, then quickly release any remaining pressure. Unlock the lid.

• Adjust the seasoning and serve.

Nutrition:

• Calories163, Total Fat 4g, Cholesterol 2mg, Sodium 955mg, Total Carbohydrate 21. 5g, Dietary Fiber 4. 6g, Total Sugars 4. 2g, Protein 12. 6g

Corn Potato Stew

• Preparation Time: 10 minutes | Cooking Time: 25 minutes | Servings: 2

Ingredients:

- 1 cup vegetable broth
- 1 cup of water
- ½ pounds potatoes, peeled, and cut into 2-inch pieces
- 1 medium onion
- ¼ teaspoon garlic powder,
- ½ teaspoons dried basil, crushed
- ½ teaspoon chili powder
- ½ teaspoon ground cumin
- ¼ teaspoon salt
- 1 cup sweet corns, rinsed and drained
- ½ cup pinto beans, rinsed and drained
- ½ tablespoon fresh cilantro

Directions:

• Add all of the ingredients to the Instant Pot and stir well.

• Cover the Instant Pot and lock it in.

• Lock the lid in place and close the steam vent.

- Set on Manual or Pressure Cooker on High Pressure for 20 minutes.
- Allow the IP to Natural-release for 5 minutes once the timer goes off.
- Remove the lid and stir to combine.
- Enjoy!

Nutrition:
- Calories358, Total Fat 2. 6g, Saturated Fat 0. 5g, Cholesterol 0mg, Sodium 710mg, Total Carbohydrate 69g, Dietary Fiber 13. 8g, Total Sugars 7. 7g, Protein 18g

Tempeh wild Rice Soup

- Preparation Time: 05 minutes | Cooking Time: 20 minutes | Servings: 2

Ingredients:

- 1 tablespoon olive oil
- 1 tablespoon coconut flour
- 2 cups vegetable broth or water
- 1cup tempeh
- ¼ cup zucchini diced
- ¼ carrot shredded
- ¼ cup uncooked wild rice
- ¼ tablespoon maple syrup
- 1 teaspoon dried mint
- 1 teaspoon kosher salt
- ½ teaspoon pepper
- 1 clove garlic minced
- 1 teaspoon cilantro chopped for garnish

Directions:

- Add broth, tempeh, zucchini, carrot, wild rice, maple syrup, mint, salt, pepper, and minced garlic to the Instant Pot and stir to combine. Lock lid, making sure the vent is closed.

- Using the display panel select the Manual or Pressure Cooker function. Use +/- keys and program the Instant Pot for 15 minutes.
- When the time is up, let the pressure naturally release for 10 minutes, then quickly release the remaining pressure.
- In a medium bowl, add coconut flour in olive oil until it makes a paste. Ladle 1 cup of the hot soup broth into the paste and stir to incorporate, then pour flour mixture into the Instant Pot.
- Using the display panel select Cancel and then Sauté. Cook and stir until thickened, then stir in the half and half.
- Serve warm topped with chopped cilantro.

Nutrition:
- Calories 356, Total Fat 17. 8g, Saturated Fat 3. 4g, Cholesterol 0mg, Sodium 1957mg, Total Carbohydrate 29. 2g, Dietary Fiber 2. 7g, Total Sugars 3. 9g, Protein 24. 3g

Pear Pumpkin Soup

• Preparation Time: 05 minutes | Cooking Time: 10 minutes | Servings: 2

Ingredients:

- ½ teaspoon butter
- ¼ onion finely diced
- 1 cup pumpkin, peeled and cubed
- 1 pear peeled and cubed
- ½ teaspoon salt
- ¼ teaspoon cumin
- ¼ teaspoon ground coriander
- 1 cup vegetable broth or water
- ½ tablespoon coconut cream
- ½ teaspoon honey

Directions:

• Add butter to the Instant Pot. Using the display panel select the Sauté function. • When butter gets melted, add onions to the Instant Pot and sauté until soft, 2-3 minutes. Add pear, salt, cumin, and spices and stir to combine.

• Add broth to the Instant Pot then add pumpkin and stir. Turn the Instant Pot off by selecting Cancel, then lock the lid, making sure the vent is closed.

• Using the display panel select the Manual or Pressure Cooker function. Use the + /- keys and program the Instant Pot for 5 minutes.

• When the time is up, quickly release the remaining pressure, then select Cancel to turn off the

pot.

• Use an immersion blender to blend the soup until smooth.

• Cool slightly, then stir in coconut cream and honey.

• Serve warm.

Nutrition:

• Calories 87, Total Fat 2. 8g, Saturated Fat 1. 6g, Cholesterol 3mg, Sodium 972mg, Total Carbohydrate 13. 3g, Dietary Fiber 2. 8g, Total Sugars 7. 4g, Protein 3. 6g

Zucchini Coconut Thai Soup

• Preparation Time: 15 minutes | Cooking Time: 20 minutes | Servings: 2

Ingredients:

- ½ tablespoon olive oil
- ½ onion, peeled and diced
- ½ pound zucchini, peeled and diced
- 1 cup spinach
- 1 small carrot
- 1 teaspoon ginger garlic paste
- ½ tablespoon red curry paste
- 2 cups vegetable broth or water
- ½ teaspoon maple syrup
- ½ cup coconut milk canned
- 1 tablespoon lime juice
- 1/4 teaspoon red pepper flakes
- 1 teaspoon of sea salt
- 1/2 teaspoon black pepper ground
- 1/4 cup basil

Directions:

• Press the Sauté button on the Instant Pot. When the display shows —Hot‖, add olive oil and heat it.

- Add the onions and carrots, zucchinis, spinach. Sauté for 3–5 minutes until onions are translucent.
- Add the ginger-garlic paste and curry paste. Continue to sauté for 1 minute.
- Add remaining ingredients, except basil. Lock lid.
- Press the Soup button and set the time to 20 minutes. When the timer beeps, let the pressure release naturally for 10 minutes. Quickly release any additional pressure until the float valve drops and then unlock the lid.
- In the Instant Pot, puree soup with a hand blender, or use a stand blender and puree in batches.
- Ladle into bowls, garnish each bowl with basil, and serve hot.
- Have fun!

Nutrition:
- Calories 136, Total Fat 7. 2g, Saturated Fat 2. 1g, Cholesterol 0mg, Sodium 1930mg, Total Carbohydrate 11. 8g, Dietary Fiber 2. 3g, Total Sugars 5. 7g, Protein 7g

Vegetable and Cottage Cheese Soup

- Preparation Time: 35 minutes | Cooking Time: 15 minutes | Servings: 2

Ingredients:

- ½ package cottage cheese, drained and cut into ¾-inch cubes
- 1 tablespoon coconut oil
- ½ teaspoon dried Italian seasoning
- 1 diced tomatoes
- 1 cup vegetable broth
- ½ cup fresh peas
- ½ cup kale
- ¼ cup cauliflower
- ½ cup 1-inch pieces green beans
- ½ cup chopped green sweet pepper
- ¼ cup sliced green olives

Directions:

- Put the cottage cheese in a plastic bag within a flat plate. Add the oil and Italian seasoning;

Turn to cover the cottage cheese. Marinate in the refrigerator for 2 to 4 hours. • Press the Sauté button on the Instant Pot. When the display shows —Hotǁ, add coconut oil and

 heat it. Press Sauté function and add cottage cheese and set timer for 5 minutes until cottage cheese browns.

• Add broth and tomato into IP. Then Add peas, kale, cauliflower, green beans, green sweet pepper, and green olives and again set the timer for 10 minutes and lock the lid of Instant Pot. • When time is up, let the pressure release naturally for 10 minutes. Quickly release any additional pressure until the float valve drops and then unlock the lid.

• Serve the soup and enjoy.

Nutrition:

• Calories229, Total Fat 12. 3g, Saturated Fat 8. 6g, Cholesterol 13mg, Sodium 765mg, Total Carbohydrate 16. 9g, Dietary Fiber 4. 5g, Total Sugars 6. 4g, Protein 15g

Zucchini Tomato Soup

- Preparation Time: 15 minutes | Cooking Time: 15 minutes | Servings: 2

Ingredients:

- 1 pound large tomatoes, cored and cut into pieces
- ¼ zucchini, cut into chunks
- ¼ cup broccoli
- 1 medium bell pepper, seeded and cut into pieces
- 1 teaspoon garlic powder
- 2 tablespoons butter, divided
- 1 tablespoon vinegar, divided
- 1 teaspoon plus a pinch of salt, divided
- ½ teaspoon plus a pinch of ground pepper, divided
- ¼ avocado
- ¼ tablespoon chopped fresh basil
- Enough water

Directions:

- Cut all the vegetables and set them aside.

• Press the Sauté mode and pour in the butter. When it melts, add zucchini, broccoli, and bell pepper and mix them. Sauté for a few minutes or until the vegetables are tender, about 5 minutes.

• Add garlic powder, water, and spices and mix.

• lock lid. Set Manual cook or Pressure for 4 minutes on High Pressure.

• Allow the IP to Natural-release for 5 minutes once the timer goes off.

• Remove the lid and mix well. Serve soup with a topping of avocado and fresh basil. • Have fun!

Nutrition:

• Calories 228, Total Fat 17. 1g, Saturated Fat 8. 4g, Cholesterol 31mg, Sodium 1266mg, Total Carbohydrate 18. 5g, Dietary Fiber 6. 1g, Total Sugars 10. 1g, Protein 4. 1g

Vegetarian Spinach Soup

• Preparation Time: 15 minutes | Cooking Time: 20 minutes | Servings: 2

Ingredients:

- ½ tablespoon coconut oil
- ¼ onion, finely chopped
- ½ stalk leek, finely chopped
- 1 teaspoon garlic powder
- 1 teaspoon basil, freshly chopped
- ¼ teaspoon red pepper flakes (optional
- Salt
- Freshly ground black pepper
- 2 cups vegetable broth
- Enough water
- 1 (15. 5oz.) can chickpea, drained and rinsed
- Juice of 1 lemon
- 1 large bunch Spinach, removed from stems and torn into medium pieces

Directions:

• In an Instant Pot press the Sauté button and set it for Medium, heat oil. Add onion, leek, and cook until slightly soft, 6 minutes. Add garlic powder, basil, and red pepper flakes and cook until fragrant, 1 minute more. Season with salt and pepper.

- Add broth, water, lemon juice, chickpea, and Spinach. Press Soup/Broth, Pressure Cooker, or Manual on High Pressure for 10 minutes with the Keep Warm setting off. The valve must be closed.
- Use the Quick-release method to return the pot pressure to normal. Unlock the lid and open the pot.
- Use an immersion blender to puree the soup right in the pot.
- Press the Sauté button and set it for Low, 250°F. Set the timer for 5 minutes.
- Bring the soup to a simmer, stirring often.
- Serve.

Nutrition:
- Calories 336, Total Fat 7. 8g, Saturated Fat 2. 7g, Cholesterol 0mg, Sodium 669mg, Total Carbohydrate 50. 7g, Dietary Fiber 15. 2g, Total Sugars 9. 8g, Protein 20. 1g

Green Soup

- Preparation Time: 10 minutes | Cooking Time: 35 minutes | Servings: 2

Ingredients:

- 4 cups vegetable broth
- 1 small onion, cut into 3/4inch pieces
- 1/3 cup rice
- 1 tablespoon vegetable oil
- 1 teaspoon garlic powder
- Salt
- 1/4 cup Greek yogurt
- 1 tsp minced fresh mint
- 1/4 tsp finely grated lime zest plus 1/2 tsp juice
- 6 oz. collard greens stemmed and chopped
- 4 oz spinach, stemmed and chopped
- 1 cup beet greens

Directions:

• Add broth, onion, rice, oil, garlic powder, and 1/2 teaspoon salt to the blender. Lock lid in place, then select Soup program 2 (for creamy soups).

• In the meantime, combine Greek yogurt, mint, lime zest and juice, and remaining 1/4 teaspoon salt in a bowl; refrigerate until ready to serve.

• Pause program 12 minutes before it has been completed. Carefully remove the lid and stir in collard greens and spinach until completely submerged.

• Return lid and resume program. Pause the program 1 minute before it has been completed. Stir in beet greens. Return lid and resume program. Once the program has completed, adjust soup consistency with extra broth as needed and season with salt and pepper to taste. Drizzle individual portions with yogurt sauce before serving.

Nutrition:

• Calories 306, Total Fat 9. 7g, Saturated Fat 1. 8g, Cholesterol 1mg 0%, Sodium 225mg, Total Carbohydrate 48. 7g, Dietary Fiber 12. 6g, Total Sugars 3. 4g, Protein 13. 6g

Tofu and Quinoa Soup

• Preparation Time: 10 minutes | Cooking Time: 20 minutes | Servings: 2

Ingredients:

• 4 ounces mushrooms, trimmed and quartered

• 1 small onion, cut into 3/4-inch pieces

• 1 1/2 tablespoons tomato paste

• 1 tablespoon olive oil

• 1 teaspoon garlic powder

• 1 teaspoon minced fresh basil

• 1/4 teaspoon pepper

• 3 cups vegetable broth

• 1 carrot, peeled and cut into 3/4-inch pieces

• 2 oz tofu and cut into ¼-inch pieces

• 1/4 cup quinoa

• 2 tablespoons minced fresh coriander

Directions:

• Microwave mushrooms, onion, tomato paste, oil, garlic powder, basil, and pepper in Instant Pot, stirring occasionally until vegetables are softened, about 5 minutes; transfer to a blender along with broth, carrot. Lock the lid in place, then select Soup Program.

• Pause program once preheating ends. Carefully remove the lid and stir in tofu and quinoa. Return lid and resume program. Once the program has completed, season with salt and pepper to taste. Sprinkle individual portions with coriander and serve.

Nutrition:

• Calories 236, Total Fat 12. 2g, Saturated Fat 1. 9g, Cholesterol 0mg, Sodium 1188mg, Total Carbohydrate 18. 6g, Dietary Fiber 3. 5g, Total Sugars 6. 7g, Protein 15. 3g

Jackfruit Beetroot Soup

• Preparation Time: 10 minutes | Cooking Time: 20 minutes | Servings: 2

Ingredients:

- 1 beetroot roughly chopped
- ½ large green turnips roughly chopped
- ½ cup jackfruit
- 2 cup water cold running tap water
- ½ teaspoon ginger powder
- 2 dried dates
- Sea salt to taste
- 2 cups of cold running tap water

Directions:

• Place all the ingredients into the Instant Pot. Pour 2 cups of cold running tap water into the pot. Do not add any salt. lock lid and pressure cook on Manual at High Pressure for 20 minutes. Turn off the heat and release it naturally (roughly 20 – 25 minutes).

• Carefully open the lid and heat the pressure cooker to bring the soup back to a full boil. Add sea salt to taste.

Nutrition:

- Calories 86, Total Fat 0. 3g, Saturated Fat 0. 1g, Cholesterol 0mg, Sodium 214mg, Total Carbohydrate 21g, Dietary Fiber 2. 6g, Total Sugars 5. 5g, Protein 2g

Quinoa Stew with Celery, Mushrooms, and Kale

- Preparation Time: 25 minutes | Cooking Time: 30 minutes | Servings: 2

Ingredients:
- ½ tablespoon coconut oil, divided
- ½ cup chopped celery
- ½ cup sliced mushrooms
- ½ teaspoon garlic powder
- 1 teaspoon minced fresh basil
- 2 tomatoes
- ½ cup quinoa
- 2 cups vegetable broth
- ½ cup kale
- 1 teaspoon chopped parsley
- Salt and pepper to taste

Directions:

• Select Sauté and adjust to Normal heat. Add the coconut oil to the Instant Pot and heat it. Add the celery sprinkle with salt and pepper. Cook, stir often until the celery softens. Add mushrooms, garlic powder, and basil and cook for about 1 minute, or until mushrooms soften. Add tomatoes and quinoa, kale, and broth.

• Lock lid in place and turn the valve to Sealing. Press the Pressure Cooker button and set the cooking time for 15 minutes at High Pressure. After cooking, let the pressure release naturally for 10 minutes, then quickly release any remaining pressure.

• Unlock the lid. Stir in the kale and stir until wilted to heat it through and thicken the sauce slightly. Taste the soup and adjust the seasoning. Ladle into bowls and sprinkle with the parsley.

Nutrition:

• Calories 263, Total Fat 7. 7g, Saturated Fat 3. 7g, Cholesterol 0mg, Sodium 800mg, Total Carbohydrate 36. 3g, Dietary Fiber 5. 3g, Total Sugars 4. 6g, Protein 13g

Butternut Squash Stew with Black Beans

• Preparation Time: 10 minutes | Cooking Time: 30 minutes | Servings: 2

Ingredients:
- ½ tablespoon butter
- ½ onion, chopped
- 1 teaspoon garlic powder
- ¼ cup butternut squash puree
- ¼ cup tomatoes
- 1 cup vegetable stock or water
- ¼ cup black beans
- ½ teaspoon cumin
- ½ teaspoon chili powder
- Salt and pepper to taste

Directions:

• Select Sauté and adjust to medium heat. Add the butter to the Instant Pot and heat until melted. Add the onion and cumin and cook, stirring often, until the onion pieces separate and soften. Add butternut squash puree, tomatoes, vegetable stock (or water), and black beans.

• Lock lid in place and turn the valve to Sealing. Press the Pressure Cooker button and set the cooking time for 10 minutes at High Pressure. After cooking, let the pressure release naturally for 20 minutes, then quickly release any remaining pressure.

• Unlock the lid. Stir in the garlic powder, chili powder, salt, and pepper and bring to a simmer, taste the beans and adjust the seasoning.

Nutrition:

• Calories 145, Total Fat 3. 6g, Saturated Fat 2g, Cholesterol 8mg, Sodium 58mg, Total Carbohydrate 23. 4g, Dietary Fiber 6. 1g, Total Sugars 3. 5g, Protein 6. 6g

Spicy Sweet Potato Stew

• Preparation Time: 10 minutes | Cooking Time: 15 minutes | Servings: 2

Ingredients:

- 1 cup vegetable broth
- ½ cup sweet potato cut into small cubes
- ½ cup pinto beans cooked, rinsed, and drained
- ½ cup red onion chopped
- ¼ cup green peas fresh or frozen
- 1 bell pepper
- ¼ teaspoon garlic powder
- 1 tomato
- 1 teaspoon red chili
- 1 teaspoon ground nutmeg

Directions:

• Place all the ingredients like sweet potato, broth, pinto beans, onion, green peas, bell pepper, garlic powder, tomato, and red chili, and nutmeg in the Instant Pot. Lock lid in place and turn the valve to Sealing. Press the Pressure Cooker button and set the cooking time for 10 minutes at High Pressure.

After cooking, let the pressure release naturally for 5 minutes, then quickly release any remaining pressure.

• Slide the steam release handle to the —Venting‖ position to release the remaining pressure until the float valve drops down.

• Remove the lid. Allow to cool 10 minutes before serving. Enjoy!

Nutrition:

• Calories 184, Total Fat 1. 7g, Saturated Fat 0. 6g, Cholesterol 0mg, Sodium 543mg, Total Carbohydrate 34. 2g, Dietary Fiber 8. 6g, Total Sugars 10. 5g, Protein 9. 7g

Broccoli Potato Soup

- Preparation Time: 05 minutes | Cooking Time: 10 minutes | Servings: 2

Ingredients:

- ½ pound broccoli
- 1 pound Yukon gold potatoes
- 2 cups vegetable broth or water
- ½ large onion
- 1 teaspoon garlic powder
- ½ tablespoons dried rosemary
- 1 cup coconut milk unsweetened

Directions:

- Place all ingredients except the coconut milk in the Instant Pot.
- Select Manual function and cook on High Pressure for 6 minutes. When time is up, release pressure.
- Add the coconut milk.
- Puree with an immersion blender right in the pot until smooth.

- This soup is delicious served over black, red, or wild rice, or alone.

Nutrition:

- Calories 148Total Fat 2. 7g, Saturated Fat 2. 1g, Cholesterol 0mg, Sodium 55mg, Total Carbohydrate 28. 8g, Dietary Fiber 5. 9g, Total Sugars 4. 4g, Protein 5. 6g

Minestrone Soup

- Preparation Time: 05 minutes | Cooking Time: 15 minutes | Servings: 2

Ingredients:

- ½ cup chickpeas cooked
- ½ cup jackfruit
- 1 sweet potato diced
- 1 zucchini diced
- ½ leek diced
- ¼ onion
- 1 teaspoon garlic, minced
- 2 cups vegetable broth
- 2 tomatoes
- 1 tablespoon Italian seasoning
- 1 teaspoon salt

Directions:

- Add all ingredients to the Instant Pot and stir. Close Instant Pot lid, and on Manual at High

Pressure, set cooking time for 15minutes.

- When time is up, let the Instant Pot release naturally for 10 minutes. Quickly release any remaining pressure.

• Serve and enjoy!

Nutrition:

• Calories 273, Total Fat 5g, Saturated Fat 0. 9g,
Cholesterol 5mg, Sodium 1969mg, Total
Carbohydrate 48. 7g, Dietary Fiber 7. 9g, Total
Sugars 10. 9g, Protein 12g

Lemon Coriander Soup

- Preparation Time: 05 minutes | Cooking Time: 15 minutes | Servings: 2

Ingredients:

- ½ tablespoon butter
- ¼ teaspoon mustard seeds
- ¼ teaspoon turmeric powder
- ½ teaspoon Pigeon peas
- ½ teaspoon red lentils
- ½ teaspoon black lentils
- 1 lemon juiced (or adjust to taste
- Salt to taste
- Water as needed for desired consistency
- 1 small bunch of cilantro or coriander
- 2 teaspoons cumin seeds
- 1 teaspoon black pepper
- 2 green chilies (or to taste
- 1 teaspoon Ginger-Garlic

Directions:

- Paste all the ingredients under —Pastell into a coarse paste without using water and keep aside. • Put Instant Pot on Sauté mode High and add butter.

- Once butter is melted add mustard seeds and turmeric powder. Fry for a minute. • Now add ground cilantro paste and fry for 2 minutes.
- Now add all three lentils and water, along with salt. Mix them well.
- Turn off Sauté mode and put the lid on. Set vent to the Sealing position.
- Do Manual High 8 mins. Do Natural-release but you can do Quick-release after 5 minutes in

Warm mode.

- After opening the lid, check for consistency, if desired add water, and put on Sauté mode for 2 to 3 minutes.
- Now add lemon juice and garnish with cilantro.
- Serve hot.

Nutrition:

- Calories73, Total Fat 5. 1g, Saturated Fat 1. 9g, Cholesterol 8mg, Sodium 227mg, Total Carbohydrate 5. 8g, Dietary Fiber 1. 3g, Total Sugars 1. 2g, Protein 1. 3g

CPSIA information can be obtained
at www.ICGtesting.com
Printed in the USA
BVHW090730230621
610212BV00009B/1052